BUILDING THE DREAM

AFFORDABLE DIY STEEL FRAME HOMES

Building the Dream: Affordable DIY Steel Frame Homes ©2024 Rodger Ford and Brad Cooper,

All rights reserved. This book or any portion thereof may not be reproduced or used in any manner whatsoever without the express written permission of the publisher except for the use of brief quotations in a book review.

ISBN: 979-8-35094-670-3

CONTENTS

Chapter 1: Meet the Team Behind Frame Up Now 1

Chapter 2: An Introduction to Affordable Steel-frame Homes 7

Chapter 3: Flowcodes, Abbreviations, and Construction Terms 11

Chapter 4: Steel-frame ADUs – the Ultimate in Adaptable, Affordable Housing 15

Chapter 5: How Steel-frame ADUs Have Become a Game-changer for the Elderly 21

Chapter 6: Building Affordable ADUs - A Family Affair 25

Chapter 7: ADUs – Ideal for Investing, Downsizing or for When Life Doesn't Go as Planned 29

Chapter 8: Steel-Frame Homes and the DIY Self-build Revolution 33

Chapter 9: Two Essential Requirements for a Home Built to Last 37

Chapter 10: Your Quick Guide to Constructing a Steel Skeleton 43

Chapter 11: FRAMECAD and FrameUpNow – the Ideal Combination 47

Chapter 12: How to Become a Steel Frame Manufacturer and Collaborator 55

Chapter 13: For those that are superstitious, there is no Chapter 13! 61

Chapter 14: A Typical FrameUpNow Set of Plans 63

Chapter 15: The FrameUpNow Collections 72

Contact Us 161

BUILDING THE DREAM

AFFORDABLE DIY STEEL FRAME HOMES

CHAPTER 1: MEET THE TEAM BEHIND FRAME UP NOW

Rodger Ford & Brad Cooper: The Founders

You may have heard of the expression "The whole is greater than the sum of its parts", and when it comes to the triumvirate responsible for the Frame Up Now concept, the phrase could not be more appropriate.

Including the two founders, we have three highly successful individuals, each from differing professional spheres, each bringing a unique set of skills to the table, yet all sharing the same common belief.

A belief in and total commitment towards cold-formed steel (CFS) frame construction for affordable residential housing, not just in the United States where the company is based, but anywhere in the world.

When three highly successful individuals each recognise the potential in a unique form of construction, yet from three separate viewpoints, you know you are on to something special.

So, let's learn a little more about the men behind the Frame Up Now concept.

Rodger Ford – A remarkable entrepreneur who is as enthusiastic about life as he enters his ninth decade as he was in his third, and who revels in identifying and developing new concepts and ideas across multiple industries. In his own lifetime he has achieved more than some would in three lifetimes, and in as diverse industries as you could imagine.

Rodger is the man who founded *AlphaGraphics, Printshops of the Future* in 1970 and which, by 1988, had expanded to 400 locations across 20 different countries.

Not content with one successful venture, Rodger also co-founded PetsHotel, which revolutionized the pet boarding industry through the provision of an upmarket sanctuary for both cats and dogs. So successful was the concept that in 2000 the company was acquired by PetsMart and today there is a PetsHotel in most PetsMart outlets.

It might well surprise you to now discover that some of Rodger's most significant and beneficial work took place in the realm of medicine, where he was the CEO of SynCardia between 2005 and 2011. There Rodger changed the operating philosophy of the company from being a 'science project' into a bioscience pioneer. The result saw the achievement of groundbreaking milestones in the realm of artificial heart technology.

Rodger spotted the potential for CFS frame construction in 2022 and his approach to the business is that of an out-of-the-box thinker, a visionary, and a man with tremendous entrepreneurial spirit and knowledge of how to effectively and efficiently bring concepts to market.

Brad Cooper – There is very little about residential construction that Brad doesn't know. Having been involved in the construction industry for 22 years, Brad is the owner of MC² Homes based in Benson, Arizona. His specialty is the construction of custom-designed properties where, as he puts it, "Each design has a meaning and a purpose."

Brad was quick to identify the many advantages of CFS frame construction and now considers it a necessity in the homes that he builds.

He spotted the potential for CFS frame construction from a practical point of view and with a constructor's eye for the whole process. While understanding how the system can be used to help construct affordable housing, he also recognised the potential for the construction of larger properties that he could offer at a more competitive price. With CFS frames there is no sacrifice in quality, but there can be considerable savings in construction time, and therefore labor costs.

Jonathon Sipe, PE

If you are looking for a highly qualified and experienced structural engineer, then you need look no further than Jonathon Sipe, PE. He is a fully licenced Structural Professional Engineer, having earned his BS/MS degrees in Structural Engineering at the University of California San Diego.

Jonathon performs structural engineering all over the US and Canada. He is licensed as a structural engineer in over 20 states, which gives him the ability to stay up to date on multiple municipality codes and requirements.

Jonathon began his career concentrating on residential property, working with major construction companies such as Lennar, KB Homes, Richmond American and Toll Brothers. From there he progressed somewhat dramatically to large-scale infrastructure projects in the sphere of bridge building, where he became highly respected and was granted several awards for new technologies and techniques he brought to the industry.

His next transition was to become heavily involved in light rail infrastructure and he has since spent the majority of his time working for some of the world's largest civil and residential engineering companies including AECOM, HDR, and WSP USA. This has allowed Jonathon the opportunity to become closely familiar with the use of both red iron and cold-form steel in the construction process.

Blessed with an innate entrepreneurial spirit and a desire to help people realize their dream homes, where he has built up a considerable reputation for his ethical business practices, Jonathon spotted the potential for CFS frames through his long-established relationship working with steel within the construction industry. As a fully qualified structural engineer, he quickly grasped the concept of cold-formed steel to create exceptional structures, knowing that as a construction material, when used correctly, steel was a highly durable and reliable material, well suited for the frame of a residential property. In turn, Jonathon also fully understood the many advantages of CFS in terms of speed of production of a steel frame, and the nature of this process that enables the creation of a wide range of property designs.

So, with three such very different skillsets brought to the table, each invaluable, it is not surprising that despite its inception only in 2022, Frame Up Now is expanding its global footprint at breakneck pace.

CHAPTER 2: AN INTRODUCTION TO AFFORDABLE STEEL-FRAME HOMES

For generations, timber has been the traditional material used in the construction of buildings, and especially residential dwellings. It is a relatively lightweight, durable and adaptable material. It is also available worldwide, even in deforested regions. Fir, such as pine and spruce are the most common forms of softwood timber used for joists, trusses, beams and posts, and most commonly for entire timber frames, primarily because it is one of the most abundant forms of wood available and because it is fast growing. A pine tree can be felled twenty years after planting, making it ideal as a sustainable material.

However, timber does have many disadvantages. You can only buy it in pre-determined lengths, and it takes time and a skilled carpenter to convert those lengths into all the necessary pieces that go to making up the frame, the structure of a property. Timber is also notorious for warping, which is a challenge in itself as timber has to season and dry out before it can be used. It can then expand if it becomes damp, and it burns all too well if there is an accidental fire in the property.

Once in place, the timber frame of a property also has to be adapted. Holes have to be drilled in it to accommodate electric cables, plumbing pipework for sanitary installations, and plumbing pipework for certain types of central heating – a time-consuming process.

Building a timber frame for a property is labor intensive, time consuming and, therefore, relatively costly.

More recently, the development of cold formed steel (CFS) has led to something of a revolution in the sphere of construction, both commercial and residential. It has proven to be an even more flexible material than wood in terms of construction design.

CFS used for the structure of a property (often called the skeleton), does not bend or warp in heat or cold. All elements of a steel-framed property come ready to use and are precision manufactured. This means that it is the ideal material for those who have competent DIY skills but who are not a trained carpenter. CFS has opened up the possibility of building your own home to many thousands of people across the globe.

It is appreciably easier and faster to assemble the structure of property with a steel skeleton or frame, meaning that considerable cost savings can be made both in terms of time and also eliminating the need for hiring skilled craftsmen. The construction plans and diagrams provided for steel skeletons provided by Frame Up Now are clearly presented so that you do not need to have years of experience in the construction industry.

Chapter 2: An Introduction to Affordable Steel-frame Homes

For the installation of all wiring and plumbing pipework, the relevant holes have been predrilled in all the steel sections which saves considerable time, while the steel will not burn in a fire. Nor is it susceptible to damage from insects, such as termites, boors, and carpenter ants, making it the ideal construction material for many a less-hospitable environment.

So, armed with the above information, it should not come as a surprise to learn that dwellings with a steel skeleton using CFS are becoming very popular for the construction of low-cost, affordable housing, and as you read on through this book, you will be able to gain a far clearer understanding of why.

CHAPTER 3: FLOWCODES, ABBREVIATIONS, AND CONSTRUCTION TERMS

Flowcodes

Steel-frame houses are revolutionizing the affordable residential building landscape, and Flowcodes are revolutionizing QR code technology. In this book we use Flowcodes, which are similar in purpose to QR codes, to direct you to additional information. Simply scan the Flowcodes with your smartphone and your smartphone will display the additional information we want you to see. We use Flowcodes because they are more reliable than traditional QR codes and are more responsive (which is better for you), giving you faster, more reliable and direct connections.

We use Flowcodes particularly for the examples of our property designs and construction details in order for you to have easy access to information you will find useful, without having to read through pages of information that isn't of use or relevant to you.

Abbreviations and Terms

For many of you, steel-frame properties may be a new concept, and with that comes new terminology. In addition, because steel-frame properties can be built by someone with competent do-it-yourself skills, there may well be a number of construction-related terms that you are also not familiar with.

While FrameUpNow is a North American company, the 25 designs it has for steel skeletons for residential properties are available worldwide. Consequently, this book tries to use generally accepted construction terms that are recognised globally.

For those of you who are simply not familiar with certain construction terms, this summary of terms and abbreviations used should prove to be very useful as you read further in this book.

Abbreviations

- **CFS – Cold-formed steel.** Cold-formed steel (CFS) Structural skeletons are made from cold, structural-quality sheet steel that are formed into C-sections and other shapes by roll forming the steel through a series of dies.

- **ADU – Accessory dwelling unit.** An accessory dwelling unit in general terms is a secondary form of residential accommodation either attached to a main residence or built on the same lot as the principal dwelling. ADUs are also referred to as 'affordable housing' and 'low-cost housing'.

- **DIY – Do It Yourself.** DIY is a shorthand term used to describe various tasks associated with property maintenance and improvement. Someone who is good at DIY should be perfectly capable of building a steel-frame property.

- **IBC – International Building Code.** This is a globally accepted standard that ensures that the quality, safety and sustainability elements of a construction project are strictly adhered to.

Terms

- **Frame –** The internal structure of a property which is attached to the foundations and to which the walls and roof are attached. Properties with a frame made from timber are referred to as timber-frame properties.

- **Skeleton** – The internal structure of a property which is attached to the foundations and to which the walls and roof are attached. The structure of a steel-frame property is more commonly referred to as a skeleton and this term is specifically used for steel frames.

- **Affordable housing** – this is a term with a different meaning to cheap housing or cheap property. Affordable housing (also known as low-cost housing) is a property constructed using lower costs than traditional properties, consequently making them more affordable to purchasers. Certain affordable or low-cost housing developments are built specifically to make inroads into the housing crisis and to provide dwellings suitable for short- and medium-term rental.

- **Low-cost dwelling** – and alternative term for affordable housing.

- **Residential property** – also referred to as a residential dwelling. The word 'residential' is used to distinguish this type of property as specifically for living in. Other types include commercial property (shops, offices, etc.) and industrial property (factories, steelworks, etc).

- **Foundations** – generally made of concrete, the foundations of a property are the ultra-stable platform on which the main structure of a property is built. Foundations are designed and constructed so that they do not move in any direction, at any time during the life of the property built on them.

- **Trusses** – invariably triangular in shape, you will find trusses on the roof of a property that provide strength and stability. The stronger the truss, the heavier the material you can cover the roof in. A truss is a web-like roof design made of steel that uses tension and compression to create strong, light components which can consequently span a long distance. The sides are in compression and the bottom is in tension to resist being pulled apart. For CFS steel-frame properties from FrameUpNow, the roof trusses will arrive on site pre-assembled to considerably reduce construction time.

- **Beams** – a beam usually runs the whole length of the property and is in one section. A roof beam is a load-bearing length of wood or steel that is integral to the strength of the building. It supports the floor or roof above while adding strength and stability to the walls. Additionally, it supports joists, trusses and other roofing elements.

- **Joists** – these are lengths of wood or steel that run perpendicular to and are supported by joists that run across open space. While beams support joists, jousts support flooring laid on the joists, or ceilings attached underneath them.

- **Wall panels** – in terms of CFS wall panels for steel-frame properties, a wall panel is part of the external structure of the property on which the roof rests. On a standard oblong, single-storey dwelling, you would have four wall panels.

Similar to steel roof trusses, wall panels for FrameUpNow steel-frame properties arrive on site pre-assembled to substantially reduce construction time.

CHAPTER 4: STEEL-FRAME ADUS – THE ULTIMATE IN ADAPTABLE, AFFORDABLE HOUSING

Is there a Difference Between ADUs and Affordable Housing?

An accessory dwelling unit (ADU) in general terms is a secondary form of residential accommodation, either connected to an existing property or built on the same lot as a principal dwelling. Because the design of ADUs varies considerably, this is the perfect scenario for Frame Up Now's cold-formed steel (CFS) system of construction, whether one of their pre-designed units or one which is made to measure.

In many countries, 'affordable housing' refers to housing units owned by housing cooperatives and associations who, in turn, rent out these properties at an affordable rent.

However, throughout this book, where we refer to affordable housing, we are simply referring to a housing unit that is affordable to build for private/personal occupation. Frame Up Now properties are described as 'affordable' as the metal frames help to substantially reduce the speed and cost of construction, making them more affordable.

If you'll excuse the pun, affordability is the foundation of CFS ADUs. However, flexibility of design is another major plus point. So, bearing in mind these two major factors, the following are ten of the most common situations identified by Frame Up Now where this type of construction is perfectly suited.

1. **A Growing Family.** In the world of residential property, it is a frequently quoted 'fact' that the three most important aspects to take into account when buying a property are location, location and location! And having found the perfect location for your home, it seems so unfair to have to leave because you have outgrown the space. Thanks to ADUs, you don't have to. Not only is the cost of construction of, say, two additional bedrooms and a shower room more affordable with a CFS steel-frame construction, but much of the cost will be covered by the saving you made in realtor's fees if you had sold your home and bought a new one.

2. **The Rising Cost of Property.** For those who are looking to get on to the property ladder, or who want to move to a larger property, the cost can be prohibitive. However, where the lot or plot is large enough, many ADUs are built within the grounds of an already

existing building. This is often the case where children have left college and are in full-time employment, but who can only afford to rent. Why pay rent when the cost of a loan to build an ADU next your parent's home will likely be so much less?

3. **Multiple Family Units.** In many societies, the family unit is what everyone lives for. Fifty years ago, in many Western societies it was rare for a family household to include grandparents and mature grandchildren who were already carving out their own careers. Today, not only will you find three generations of adults under one roof, but you will often find great grandchildren as well. Many traditional homes just do not have the space needed for multiple families, but the addition of one or two ADUs within the grounds of the existing home can solve all accommodation problems, whether these units are attached to the main property, or are detached and self-contained.

4. **Divorce**. It is an unfortunate fact of life that after a divorce, there often comes a dramatic change in lifestyle, and especially the home you live in. This period can be especially difficult for women who have young children, and they are the principal carer. However, for husbands and wives, building an ADU in the grounds of your parent's home can provide you not just with affordable accommodation of a good standard, but you also have a child support network next door!

5. **Unemployment or a Change in Employment**. Being made unemployed can cause a financial crisis and if you have a substantial mortgage to pay, your home could also be at risk. However, if you have owned your home long enough, you could sell it (while retaining sufficient land to build an ADU on it) and use the net proceeds after any mortgage has been paid off to go towards the cost of your ADU. The same can apply if you want to change careers but

feel tied to your current job because you have a large mortgage to pay. Building and then living in an ADU for a few years could give you the financial freedom to pursue a whole new career.

6. **Caring for Elderly Parents.** One of the biggest challenges when wanting to care for elderly parents is their desire not to surrender their independence. In addition, they may have downsized earlier in life and their current home would be impractical for two families or a carer to live in. An ADU, whether an independent structure or attached to the principal dwelling could be a complete game-changer. Building on a self-contained ADU for a carer would see parents retain their independence, yet also have help on hand for whenever needed.

7. **Lack of Affordable Housing.** In certain cities there is such a shortage of building land and such high demand for property, that for a first purchase, the cost of anything other than a broom closet is just too high. It is not so much your children don't want to leave home; they just can't afford a place of their own.

Depending on your own financial circumstances, you might be able to afford to construct an ADU for them to live in while they save money for the deposit on a place of their own, or alternatively they could perhaps afford a loan to build an ADU but would never have been able to afford the money for a plot of land as well.

8. **Investment.** If you live in an area where there is good rental demand, and particularly in an area where the value of residential property is very high, why not build an ADU on your own land. Many planning restrictions are being lifted owing to a lack of residential homes in large cities. Investing in an ADU could give you a very good return on your investment and as it would be a brand-new property, your maintenance costs would be negligeable.

9. **A DIY Home-build Project.** There has been a dramatic increase in the number of people who decide to build their own home, and this can be put down to one very clear reason. YouTube. Yes, that may surprise you, but when it comes to building your own home, there is a YouTube video (and often many of them) for every single aspect of property construction, from laying foundations to changing a light bulb. The greatest problem facing DIY home builders was the timber frame, which required exceptional carpentry skills. With that replaced by the simplicity of construction with a Frame Up Now CFS steel frame, not only is it easier to build your own home, but it is now more affordable as well.

10. **DIY Community Self-build Projects.** Across the globe there are small pockets of five or six houses that have been built by a group of tradesmen who have shared their skills, in a form of bartering, to build a family home they would not have otherwise been able to afford. Put together a plumber and electrician, a carpenter, a drywaller, a construction specialist and a roofer and you would be surprised what can be achieved. With the introduction of CFS steel frames, these projects have been speeded up considerably, while costs have again been lowered. Members of these community groups all still work full time, but then spend their evenings, weekends and holidays working on each other's properties until they have all been completed.

There is one more thing we should add, which we feel is very important. In many major urban areas, there is a problem with homelessness. Whether through divorce, being made unemployed, or through simply being unable to break the cycle of needing a permanent address to get work, there is a need for more ADUs to help these individuals. Whether you class it as philanthropy, social responsibility or sensible investing, the more ADUs that can be added to the urban landscape, the greater the chance of reducing the problem of homelessness.

As you can see, the opportunities for affordable steel-framed houses are endless, and these opportunities all share one common bond – making property ownership as flexible and affordable to as many people as possible.

CHAPTER 5: HOW STEEL-FRAME ADUS HAVE BECOME A GAME-CHANGER FOR THE ELDERLY

For many who enter their 'golden years', retaining independence is often seen as a benchmark for how good life is. However, with the rapid growth in house prices, many first-time buyers are having to turn their parents for financial aid to help them get a foot on the property ladder. So, the passing of time brings with it a whole new set of challenges that need to be met and hurdles that must be overcome. Thanks to FrameUpNow and FRAMECAD, steel-frame affordable housing now provides multiple solutions, many not previously thought of or possible, for the majority of these problems and challenges if the plot or yard your current home occupies is large enough.

Let us look at five of the most common situations faced by the elderly where an ADU (accessory dwelling unit), also known as affordable housing, would work well and would avoid you having to relocate or move home.

1. **Becoming infirm** – It is wrong to assume that once your health begins to deteriorate, that the only option available is to move into a nursing or care home, or assisted housing where there is help available 24/7. Why not build an ADU for a 'live-in' carer. It could be a totally independent unit, or it could be attached to your home with an interconnecting door. Not only will you add value to your home, but you will also save a fortune in nursing home / care home fees.

2. **Bringing your family closer to you** – Of course, you could achieve two goals with one project. If you are struggling to look after yourself and your home, perhaps it is now too big for you to maintain, why not build an independent ADU. Then, if your son or daughter has a family and they already live nearby, they could move into the main house and look after you, while you still retain your pride and keep your independence in your own, smaller property. A good accountant will advise you, but where estate planning is concerned; you may choose to sell the main house to your son or daughter at a reduced price (to cover the cost of your ADU) or gift the property to them as part of your legacy.

3. **Boost your pension fund** – It could be that most of your wealth is tied up in your home. This is quite a common situation. You could consider building an affordable home on the plot and then rent out the main house to generate a monthly income. Alternatively, if you have modest savings, an affordable steel-framed home built within the boundary of your property could be let out to generate additional income. The property would become even more affordable to build as you will only have to pay for the structure – you already own the land it will be built on!

4. **Helping out your family, financially** – In many countries, the value of property has risen so much in the last twenty years that

getting on the property ladder can be very difficult, if not impossible. Because the younger generation have so many options available where work is concerned, many choose to live in a town or city a long way from home, and sometimes even abroad. Local planning laws may allow you to build an independent ADU on the existing plot of your home, create an independent entrance, and then you could sell off the main home. The proceeds would comfortably pay for your ADU and allow you to help your children buy rather than rent a property.

5. **Staying with your family** – It may be tradition where you live that the family stays together and all under the same roof. That may have worked out well when it is you, your wife and two children. Once they get married and started their own families, it is likely space will become a premium. Then, when their children become teenagers and require their own bedrooms, you may then be forced to look at the costly option of moving to a larger property or they may have to consider living elsewhere. However, with the low cost of construction, you could easily expand the square footage of the existing property with steel-framed extensions to provide additional bedrooms and living space. If you work out the finances involved, you will find this is one of the most financially viable options.

And what are the two things all of the above five scenarios have in common?

First, each option has added capital value to the principal residence. This makes perfect sense if you have children you wish to leave a legacy to.

Second. There is no relocation. No changing towns, no saying goodbye to neighbours, no massive upheaval at a time in life when you least need it.

An ADU makes perfect sense in so many different ways.

CHAPTER 6: BUILDING AFFORDABLE ADUs - A FAMILY AFFAIR

In this book we have discussed the multiple benefits of building an ADU when you become less able to look after yourself but are still keen to retain your independence. All those options apply when you already own a property. However, there are numerous other scenarios where, as a homeowner, building an ADU or affordable housing unit on your property would still make a lot of sense if the property you own is on a sufficiently large plot.

And if you are wondering why ADUs or affordable housing can provide so many solutions to a myriad challenges and problems, the answer, to a degree, lies in the description. Steel-frame homes have already carved themselves a niche in today's property market, not just in the U.S. the UK or Europe, but across the entire globe because they are providing a cost-effective solution to many of today's housing problems.

Now, if a property is affordable to build and that affordability includes the price of the lot or plot the property is built on, imagine just how much more affordable a steel-framed home would be when you already own the land! So, what scenarios are we talking about here?

1. **Helping your children gain their independence** – In many countries the average age for children leaving home and buying their own property is now well over 30. The sole reason for this is the rising price of residential property in areas where there are good work opportunities. With many mature children looking to gain their independence, only achieved by leaving home, they run the risk of falling into a common trap. If you can't buy your own home and get on the property ladder, then your only option is to rent one. However, with

the rising value of residential property, so rents have risen, and renting a property is now so costly, it is impossible to also save for a deposit in order to buy a property later on. What is paid in rent just becomes 'lost money'.

As a parent. You have two options if you want to help out your children and allow them to become more independent. If your savings permit, you could build an ADU within the plot of your current property and let your son or daughter live in the ADU while they save up enough money for a place of their own. You could alternatively downsize your own property and build an ADU in the grounds of your new, smaller home. Once your child or children have saved enough money to buy their own property, you can then let out the ADU and boost your retirement fund!

In the ideal scenario, once your son or daughter has become financially stable with a secure job, they could well decide to buy the ADH you had built from you and get on the property ladder that way.

And if they do save up enough money to buy their own property elsewhere, you will be able to boost your income by letting out the ADU and get a very good return on the capital you have invested.

2. **Children's divorce** – There is the scenario where, unfortunately, one of your children gets divorced. One of the biggest challenges facing divorced couples is that one or both have to find somewhere else to live. If there are children involved, in the majority of situations, the mother becomes the primary caregiver and, therefore, she will require more space. In a perfect world that would mean continuing to live in the family home, especially as it would then minimize disruption for young children who are faced with an emotionally challenging time.

Unfortunately, we do not live in a perfect world.

The problem is, life begins to look somewhat 'unfair' when you realise that property values are such that the value of a three-bedroom family home is likely about twice the price of a one-bedroom apartment, which creates problems where the children are concerned.

If, financially, the only option available is to sell the family home, then what can be done about finding new homes for both parties, and the children? After all, as an adult, returning home to live with your parents is seen as a last resort as somehow, having left home, returning tends to create a sense of failure.

For the one who will be the primary caregiver to the children, remaining in the family home may not be possible as they may not have the ability to take over the existing mortgage, even with financial aid from their ex-partner.

Similarly, even for the partner who is not the primary caregiver, providing financial support can make paying a hefty mortgage on a new property for themselves particularly challenging. However, ADUs could be a complete 'gamechanger' for one if not both parties involved, especially if parents can help in providing space on the plot of their own home to build an ADU.

ADUs are called affordable homes for a reason and when speed of construction is combined with affordability, they can be the perfect solution to housing problems following a marriage or relationship break-up.

CHAPTER 7: ADUs – IDEAL FOR INVESTING, DOWNSIZING OR FOR WHEN LIFE DOESN'T GO AS PLANNED

There are no hard and fast rules that say who or why you can live in an affordable property, an ADU (accessory dwelling unit). Consequently, in this book we have looked to mention only the most likely scenarios where affordable housing can provide a viable option for many of the residential hurdles encountered in life. To a degree, the adaptability and versatility of steel-frame ADUs make them the 'Swiss army knife' of the domestic construction world.

This section of the book will deal with two key areas where affordable housing can play an important role, though from very different perspectives, change in financial circumstance and as an investment.

Investing in an affordable housing unit, an ADU

Traditionally, property has always been seen to be a good long-term investment. The trouble is, today, for many, the cost of event the cheapest property puts it out of reach where investing is concerned.

Where steel-frame low-cost housing is concerned, while the cost of construction may be a lot less than traditional construction methods, that doesn't mean the rental income will also be less than for a traditionally built equivalent. Ordinarily you might look for a 6-9% return on capital invested when setting the rent on a traditional property is concerned. If you can charge the same rent for a property that costs less to build, then it makes a steel-frame affordable home an even better investment.

However, there is one word that perfectly sums up steel-frame homes through FrameUpNow and that is 'versatility'. Beyond the twenty-five designs we offer, there is still the option to create purpose-built ADUs that can meet local market demand.

With there being a homelessness crisis in many cities worldwide, there is huge demand for the most elementary forms of accommodation - a bed-sitting room with an integral kitchenette, and a separate shower/toilet/bathroom. Whether individual 'pods' or creating a structure with multiple units, investing in low-rent affordable homes could not just generate regular income with high demand, but you will also be contributing to a solution for the homeless problem. It should be noted that many homeless people are not unemployed nor have mental health problems, they just live in a city where rents have skyrocketed, and they are simply unable to afford even a one-bedroom flat or a room to rent in an HMO (house of multiple occupancy).

Beyond being able to build properties that are designed to meet the demands of a local rental market, there is another big plus when it comes to building and renting out an ADU – brand-new properties require next to no maintenance. In other words, you won't be spending half your rental income fixing things!

Downsizing to an ADU

Often, when retiring, many parents find their current home too large. It was perfect for bringing up a family, but if everyone has left home, why spend so much money maintaining a property that is not fully occupied? Instead, why not sell your home, buy a new, smaller one or, better still, build your own steel-framed home to your perfect design, and build a second ADU with the remainder of the sale proceeds from the family home to bring you in extra income? The advantage of investing in an ADU is that you not only get a return on capital through rent, which is appreciably more than you will get if the money was earning interest in a savings account, but you should also get an increase in the value of your ADU over time as property traditionally increases in value in the long term.

A Change in Financial Circumstances

It is an unfortunate fact that today we no longer live in a world where 'a job is for life' as it was back in our grandparents' day. So, what happens if you lose your job and can't pay the mortgage, or any other loan secured on your home? Well, thanks to FrameUpNow and affordable steel-frame homes, the situation needn't be as dire as it might first seem.

If you have lived in your property for a good few years, chances are if you sell it, you could release a good chunk of capital that would enable you to pay off any loan and 'temporarily' downsize by building a steel-frame home, helping to keep your foot on the property ladder and avoid throwing money down the drain by paying rent.

By keeping your money invested in property, when your financial situation changes, you then have the option of moving home again, or as is becoming a popular option, you just get a new steel-frame extension designed and increase the size of your existing steel-frame home.

CHAPTER 8: STEEL-FRAME HOMES AND THE DIY SELF-BUILD REVOLUTION

With the introduction of steel-frame affordable housing, more and more people today are choosing to build their own home. By that, we mean adopting a hands-on approach to the construction process as opposed to supervising a team of construction professionals. While there have always been a small minority of people who have chosen to build their own home, though usually they already had very competent DIY skills and a lot of knowledge – invariably having worked at one time or another in the construction industry.

Why self-build is becoming such a popular option

However, today, the landscape has changed from thirty years ago, and there are four principal reasons for this revolution in the self-build community:

Rising property prices

First, property prices have risen to the extent where, for many, it is just too expensive to buy a property that meets all your needs. This has inspired many individuals to explore the possibility of building their own property as a less costly alternative. There is a reason why ADUs are also referred to as affordable housing… because they allow more and more people to become homeowners who, under most circumstances, can only afford to waste money on rent.

The arrival of steel-frame skeletons

Second, there is the arrival of the steel-frame home. Thanks to developing technology and the massive progress made in terms of production technology, it is now possible to buy a steel frame, or skeleton as it is known, for any number of pre-designed residential properties. For example, at FrameUpNow we have over 60 designs for 'ready to order' frames. Previously, one of the biggest hurdles to building your own property was having the necessary carpentry and brick- or block-laying skills, together with knowledge and experience to build the frame of the property, that part to which everything else is attached – the roof, the walls, internal partitions, flooring, etc. Today, these steel skeletons come ready for assembly together with clear drawings and precise instructions, enabling anyone with competent DIY skills to assemble a steel skeleton. Better still, with the creation of a global network of manufacturing outlets where the parts for the frame are produced, you can order your frame through FrameUpNow, which is based in the U.S.A. and have it manufactured just a few miles down the road, whether you live in the Americas, Europe, Africa, Asia or the Far East, dramatically reducing shipment costs. At FrameUpNow we are genuinely doing all we can to make steel-frame properties as affordable as possible.

Affordable and effective power tools

Third, we have the dramatic improvements in and lowering of the cost of power tools. It is not that long ago that many building tasks were carried out manually, and by that we mean sawing, sanding, nailing, drilling, mixing concrete, etc. Today, there is a power tool for virtually every manual task. Not only does this reduce the skill level required, but it also speeds up the construction process, dramatically. With more and more people becoming DIY enthusiasts, the price of many of these power tools has fallen, making them far more affordable, and if you don't have a DIY superstore near you, there are plenty of online options for home delivery.

YouTube how-to videos and the internet

 Fourth, no longer do we need the knowledge or have to speak to friends who are in the construction business to learn about building a property. Today, you can go on YouTube, type in "How to …." And you will have a fantastic choice of videos to watch. Whether it is plumbing or wiring a house, fitting a bath or sink, tiling walls or floors, decorating, insulating, drywalling or plaster boarding, etc., you will have many, many videos to choose from. The list is endless, and these videos will also go into the more intricate details, such as 'How to fit a tap', 'How to fit a door hinge', 'How to mix concrete'.

YouTube has an active DIY community where you can interact with creators, ask questions, and share your own DIY experiences. You can leave comments, join discussions, and even connect with like-minded DIY enthusiasts. So, if you encounter a problem, there will always be someone around to give you advice.

Beyond YouTube, having access to the internet and using a search engine such as Google will provide you with answers to may other construction process queries. For example, you can look for "what ratio of sand and cement do I need to make mortar", or, if you wish to be as eco-friendly as possible with the construction, you can search for "eco-friendly insulation". There really isn't much you can't find out about building a property on the internet these days. What we would say though, is to be thorough in your research and cross-check the information you get, especially on Google searches as often information provided is 'opinion based' as opposed to verified by facts.

See for yourself

 Here we have only scratched the surface with regard to what is involved with a self-build project. However, we thought you might like to see how a FrameUpNow steel skeleton is erected, so just use the flow code below.

CHAPTER 9: TWO ESSENTIAL REQUIREMENTS FOR A HOME BUILT TO LAST

For many of you who are reading this book, by the time you have finished, you may well be ready to embark on a venture you might not have dared imagine ten years ago – building your own home. While this book is also for the guidance of those who already work in the construction industry, we wanted to include those of you who have sound do-it-yourself (DIY) skills. The cold-formed steel (CFS) frame, or skeleton for ADUs (accessory dwelling units) or affordable housing is easy to erect and thanks to the plethora of YouTube videos on the 'net, there is nothing in the realm of property construction, from laying foundations to plumbing in a sink that doesn't have a selection of 'how to' videos to watch, and in every language imaginable! You don't need the knowledge, just a basic skillset and access to the internet to be able to build your own steel-frame home!

In reality, there is something of a revolution occurring in the construction industry across the globe with steel-frame skeletons enabling more and more of you to build your own home, and at a price appreciably more affordable than buying a traditionally built property from a developer – one of the main reasons steel-frame properties are becoming so popular.

So, what are the two essential requirements of a home built to last?

In simple terms, a solid frame, or skeleton (what you build) and firm foundations (on what you build).

The Frame or Skeleton

To avoid any confusion, properties with a main structure made of timber are referred to as timber-frame properties. Where cold-formed steel (CFS) is concerned, the CFS frame in a property is referred to as a skeleton. Both structures fulfil the exact same purpose – they provide a solid structure around which you build the walls, roof and fit out the interior.

Multiple Advantages of a CFS skeleton

Timber is prone to bending and warping under extreme conditions such as high or low temperatures, excessive moisture or high winds. CFS does not suffer from any of these drawbacks.

Timber is subject to attack from dry and wet rot, woodworm, termites, boors, carpenter ants and various other insects. CFS is impervious to all such attacks and infestations.

Timber is flammable and in a fire is likely to aid in the total destruction of a property. CFS in non-combustible and can help to retard the spread of a domestic fire.

As a result of the above, insurance companies rate CFS-framed properties lower than timber-framed ones, thus lowering your insurance premiums.

International acceptance

Part of the reason for the global spread of FRAMECAD steel-frame housing is the international standards which it meets. The CFS skeletons we provide at FrameUpNow are designed to International Building Code (IBC) Standards. The IBC is responsible, globally, for ensuring that the quality, safety and sustainability elements of a construction project are strictly adhered to. All 60 FrameUpNow steel-frame skeleton designs meet the IBC standard.

All FrameUpNow skeletons are delivered with an IBC stamp of approval.

The Foundations

If the foundations of a building are not rock solid, then it doesn't matter how stable the skeleton or frame of a property is: the property won't last and at best will be unsafe to live in.

It is no coincidence that in life we refer to so many things requiring 'solid foundations', though in most instances we are talking figuratively, not literally. Anything built on a solid foundation, whether literally or figuratively, will last much longer.

The foundations to a property perform two functions. They ensure that the property does not sink into the ground when built – you would be surprised just how much a house weighs! Second, they help to evenly distribute the weight of the property across the ground to optimize stability.

Hire a professional for this stage of construction

 There is no 'one size fits all' type of foundations. Foundations for a property built on rock differ from those for a property built on clay soil, or sandy soil. For this reason, we strongly recommend you employ the services of an architect or structural engineer to carry out tests on the land the property will be built on.

They will also check for groundwater levels and seismic activity and provide you with detailed drawings (plans) of the most appropriate foundations for the property you wish to build.

Once you are in receipt of these plans, you should then hire a professional contractor to lay the foundations. They will have comprehensive knowledge relating to site preparation, formwork, concrete mixing, pouring, finishing, and curing.

Get official paperwork to guarantee the work on your foundations

There are two reasons we recommend you employ professionals to build the foundations of your property. First, you will have peace of mind that your property has been built on 'solid ground' while also giving you the right to legal recourse (insurance) if anything goes wrong. Second, and more important, you are protecting the value of your 'investment'.

There may come a time when you need to sell on your steel-frame property. Depending on where you live, the value of the property can be affected if there is no paperwork to prove that the property has been built to the standards required by local building regulations/authorities. In many instances, banks or building societies will not lend money to the purchaser of a property if it lacks the required paperwork and plans to prove that everything meets all required regulations.

It is also worth noting that that if you do decide to build the property yourself and intend to do the wiring and plumbing yourself, it will also pay to have a registered electrician and registered plumber check and 'sign off' all your work to show that it has all been installed to the correct specifications. Note also that in many countries, it is against the law to install plumbing and fires/furnaces/boilers that involve gas unless you are fully trained and qualified.

In other words, in several instances, while the costs of building a steel-framed property are lower than a traditionally built one, there are certain corners you cannot afford to cut or you could end up affecting its value or, where appropriate, its saleability!

What is included in foundation plans?

Without foundation plans, the contractor you employ to lay the foundations will have no idea what is required of them.

Foundation plans may vary, depending on where you live, but can include any or all of the following:

- Foundation Layout
- Footings
- Foundation Walls
- Columns and Piers
- Foundation Materials
- Floor Elevation Drainage Details
- Site Information

Three types of foundations

There are generally three types of foundations used in residential construction, which can be modified based on local terrain conditions:

- Shallow foundations
- Deep foundations
- Combined foundation systems

Get the foundations and the frame right, and you can build a property that will last a lifetime and beyond.

CHAPTER 10: YOUR QUICK GUIDE TO CONSTRUCTING A STEEL SKELETON

Before beginning the construction of your steel skeleton, we strongly recommend you purchase all the appropriate safety equipment for working on a construction site. This should include safety boots and safety goggles or glasses, a hard hat, a high-visibility jacket and ear defenders for when using noisy power tools.

There is a wealth of information available on the internet for health and safety on a construction site, most of which is basic common sense. Our principal piece of advice is to always keep the site clean and tidy. When building a dwelling, we tend to spend more time looking ahead or upwards than down at our feet, so best to make sure nothing is left lying around that anyone could trip over. As an added bonus, a clean site is also more efficient to work in.

The following are the seven steps you will need to take in the construction of your new steel-frame dwelling. For each of these sections we have provided a summary of what will be required, and each flowcode will give you access to more comprehensive, invaluable information.

The right tools for the job – included in the information you will be provided when you purchase the plans for a steel-frame dwelling will be a comprehensive list of tools you will need to complete the entire construction process. However, for the frame erection stage, there is only a very short list as the main task will be to connect the individual pieces of the frame together.

Make sure you have the right tools for the job as your frame is the most important part of the dwelling's entire structure.

 **Site preparation and laying the foundations** – here we recommend you use professional contractors. First the site needs to be cleared and then surveyed in order to establish what type of foundations will be needed. Then the site is cleared, ready for the concrete base and any foundation trenches to be dug where necessary.

Note that any services (water, gas, electricity and drainage) need to be installed in advance of laying the foundations, so that when the foundations are laid, you will have direct connections to them all through the concrete base.

 **Get your snaplines right** – once your concrete foundations have dried, you need to mark out where the frame is going to sit. You can establish the precise location based on the position of all the connections to the utilities as you will know exactly, based on the plans, where in the dwelling each of these will be connected.

The next step is to create snaplines on the concrete. These are called snaplines as it requires two of you to run a length of heavily chalked string along the concrete base where the outside of the wall frame will be. You then tighten the string, lift it up and allow it to snap back into place – leaving a nice clear and straight line of chalk on the concrete. This needs to be done for all external wall frames and it is important to ensure that all lines are at 90 degrees (a right angle) to each other.

 **Taking delivery of the steel frame** – all the wall frames, beams, trusses and joists will arrive on the back of a lorry. As you unload them, check that everything is in the right order. In theory, the last thing to come off the lorry should be the first piece you will use when you start the construction process. In simple terms, you want all the pieces stacked sequentially to match the order of installation.

Chapter 10: Your Quick Guide to Constructing a Steel Skeleton

 Get on the phone and invite a load of (capable) friends round to a frame construction party. Four or five people will be enough depending on the overall size of the frame, and this is a great way to make building your new home even more memorable and enjoyable.

 **Installing wall panels** – If you've got your snaplines right, installing and connecting all the wall panels together could not be easier or more straightforward.

 **Cross bracing** – cross bracing is installed to provide extra stability to keep the panels square to each other, and to stop them from racking.

 **Installing the trusses** – once your wall panels are in place, you are now ready to install the roof trusses. Depending on their size, you may be able to manually lift them into place, but for larger and heavier trusses, mechanical machinery will be needed.

Time for an impromptu barbecue and a celebratory drink of something fizzy!

Once you have watched the videos that show how simple and rapid it is to erect a steel skeleton, you should feel confident that you definitely have the DIY skills to build your own home.

CHAPTER 11: FRAMECAD AND FRAMEUPNOW – THE IDEAL COMBINATION

The Vision: Mark Taylor, Founder of FRAMECAD, "My vision for the FRAMECAD User Network is to create the world's most productive affordable housing network with a common platform which enables the ability to *centralize and perfect design*, yet 'print' certified high-quality cold-formed steel skeletons in close proximity to the chosen construction site."

FrameUpNow: has the experience, knowledge, skills and technology to *centralize and perfect the design* of residential properties, with a strong emphasis on affordable housing.

Today, the FrameUpNow design center has created and perfected a library of 60 designs for residential units with full construction plans, thus simplifying the greatest challenge to the construction process.

Additionally, FrameUpNow has a curated Library that beyond residential property, has design specifications for multiple non-residential buildings/structures, from small as shops or garages to large multiple-purpose barndominiums – a new design based on an old theme where a residential property is integrated within a large barn or workshop.

The FrameUpNow designs can be electronically transferred to one of the thousands of FRAMECAD manufacturing units located in over 120 countries so that affordable home steel skeletons or frames can be 'printed off' virtually on site, almost anywhere in the world.

About FRAMECAD

FRAMECAD, a global leader in cold-formed steel (CFS) construction, represents one of the biggest transformations seen in the construction industry for decades. Founded by Mark Taylor in 1987 in New Zealand, FRAMECAD, has grown into a leading force for innovation, efficiency, cost-effectiveness and sustainability.

The Genesis of FRAMECAD

Mark Taylor, laid the foundation for FRAMECAD in the serene landscapes of New Zealand, initially focusing on roofing products, Taylor's vision was to redefine, simplify and speed up construction using cold-formed steel. This vision initiated a construction revolution.

Embracing Cold-formed Steel

The adoption of cold-formed steel marked a significant shift. Known for its strength and resilience, it addressed environmental and efficiency concerns in traditional construction. FRAMECAD's technology harmonized with this material, optimizing every construction phase.

The FRAMECAD Building System

FRAMECAD's system is a symphony of design and efficiency. It encompasses the interplay of aesthetics and functionality in design, precision in manufacturing, and streamlined construction, significantly reducing building times and environmental impact.

FRAMECAD's Global Impact - FRAMECAD's technology extends globally, offering sustainable building solutions in disaster-affected areas. It has been instrumental in constructing emergency housing, schools, and hospitals, showcasing adaptability in even the most challenging environments.

FRAMECAD's Vision for the Future - FRAMECAD aims to pioneer sustainable building practices and expand into emerging markets. Its ambition goes beyond conventional construction, shaping the future of global construction. With over 1,000 FRAMECAD 'printing' systems in the market in over 120 countries, FRAMECAD aims to create the world's most productive affordable homes network with a common platform which provides the capability of designing a property anywhere yet 'printing' a certified, high-quality steel frame or skeleton close to the building site.

FRAMECAD in Affordable Housing - FRAMECAD now plays a crucial role in affordable housing. Its technology used in residential construction offers numerous advantages, including speed, design flexibility, building quality and low cost, making it a viable solution for affordable housing.

Advantages of Using FRAMECAD in ADUs

Rapid Construction: One of the primary advantages of FRAMECAD in constructing accessory dwelling units (ADUs) is the significant reduction in construction time. FRAMECAD's automated design and manufacturing process streamlines construction, enabling faster completion of housing units without compromising quality. In this section of the book, we will discuss the positive implications of rapid construction for affordable housing projects, including how it enables quicker occupancy and reduces overall project costs.

Durability and Resilience: Durability and resilience are critical in affordable housing construction. FRAMECAD's cold-formed steel structures offer enhanced durability and resilience against environmental challenges. In this section of the book, we will discuss the material properties of CFS that contribute to the longevity and maintenance-free nature of FRAMECAD-constructed ADUs, ensuring they are safe, built to last, and require minimal upkeep.

Cost-Effectiveness: Affordability is a key concern in addressing the global housing crisis. The efficiency of FRAMECAD's system results in significant cost savings, particularly in the context of ADU construction. This section of the book will analyze how FRAMECAD reduces material waste, labor costs, and overall construction expenses, making the development of ADUs more economically viable.

Environmental Sustainability: Sustainability is integral to FRAMECAD's approach to construction. This section of the book will examine the environmental benefits of using FRAMECAD in ADU construction, focusing on its role in promoting green building practices. By reducing construction waste, optimizing material usage, and improving energy efficiency, FRAMECAD contributes to more sustainable construction practices.

Introduction to FRAMECAD Cold-formed Steel

- **The FRAMECAD System** stands out as a world leader in cold-formed steel (CFS) construction, offering unmatched efficiency and quality in the industry. Its integration of engineering and design software positions it as a top choice, globally, for premium and low-cost residential construction projects.

- **FRAMECAD's Design-led Construction Approach**, specifically with cold-formed steel framing, significantly reduces overall residential project costs. It enables a faster construction process, up to 75% quicker than traditional methods, and allows for more internal space in single dwellings due to narrower walls.

- **Advantages in Affordable Homes:** For single dwellings, the versatility of CFS is ideal, especially in urban areas where there is high density of dwellings and design flexibility is key. The FrameUpNow solutions are cost-effective, offering swift construction, which are both crucial for meeting the world's ever-increasing housing demands.

- **Sustainability and Energy Efficiency:** CFS aligns with global sustainability and energy efficiency goals, being 93% recyclable. It supports green building practices and enables the integration of energy-efficient systems, thus reducing residential energy consumption. CFS construction also generates less waste compared to traditional construction methods.

- **Design Versatility and Construction Efficiency:** CFS offers unparalleled design versatility, accommodating larger span lengths and innovative architectural designs that a timber frame struggles to provide. The precise manufacturing of steel components allows for quicker installation and optimizes material usage. Moreover, steel framing requires fewer workers for assembly, once again reducing labor costs and accelerating construction speed.

- **Cold-formed Steel in Offsite Construction**: Cold-formed steel is particularly suitable for offsite construction, allowing for simultaneous construction activities. Its lightweight nature eases onsite handling, reducing the need for heavy equipment. This efficiency contributes to a faster construction speed and compresses overall project timelines, leading to a quicker return on investment where needed.

FRAMECAD and FrameUpNow: and cold-formed steel are not just a solution; they represent a transformation in how we approach affordable housing, combining speed, efficiency, sustainability, affordability and innovation to address the critical challenges of our time.

With FRAMECAD manufacturing technology and FrameUpNow design-led manufacturing solutions, the future of affordable homes has never looked more promising.

CHAPTER 12: HOW TO BECOME A STEEL FRAME MANUFACTURER AND COLLABORATOR

This informative book is not intended solely for potential homeowners of affordable steel-frame skeletons (frames). There may well be many of you out there with an entrepreneurial spirit and a keen eye for an exciting and financially rewarding business opportunity and you may currently be a home builder or framer using timber. Alternatively, you may be in the business of supplying lumber and pre-constructed panels and trusses to home builders.

Producing steel frames yourself

So, welcome to the rapidly expanding world of manufacturing steel-frame houses!

Here at FrameUpNow we are in the process of creating a regional and global network of manufacturers of steel-frame properties using the

FRAMECAD and FrameUpNow systems. The following will give you a quick insight into why we are doing this.

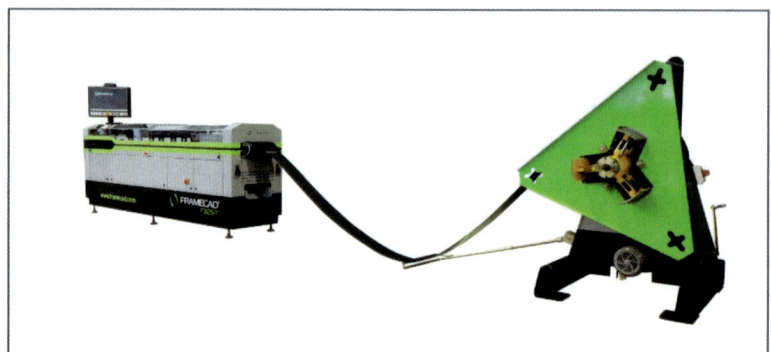

Small footplate The FRAMECAD system is quite remarkable. The F325iT-L, which is suitable for producing steel frames for residential construction, has a footplate of no more than 4m x 0.8m (13' x 3') and a height of around 1.2m (4.0') for the main body

Impressive production rates

Seeing it in action is even more impressive and you will struggle not to be both impressed and amazed at just how clever this machinery is. It can take a roll of 21-18 gauge (0.75mm – 1.22mm) cold-formed steel (CFS) and produce profiles (individual elements of the steel frame) with a width of between 63mm – 150mm (2.5" – 6.0") at a rate of 300m/hr (985' ft/hr) for joists and 700m/hr (2,300ft/hr) for wall panels.

Digital Instruction

The purchaser of a FrameUpNow steel-frame skeleton also buys a set of digital instructions for the manufacture of the steel frame. These instructions are held in a one-time-only-use file which is sent to their nearest FRAMECAD manufacturer. The digital file instructs the F325iT-L to produce every part that ultimately joins together and becomes the wall panels, trusses, beams and floor joists for that specific steel structure.

Grow your own CFS business, whether in the U.S.A. or anywhere in the world

Are you currently building residential homes, or do you supply panels and trusses to builders?

Are you constructing twenty-plus units a year where switching to steel-frame construction could well make financial sense and be a game-changer? Can you see the bigger picture yet?

Once you start building units with steel frames, people are going to notice, and other builders are going to notice the speed at which you are now producing new homes. Next thing you know, they're going to be asking you where you get your frames from. Because you have invested in your own FRAMECAD system, let's say the F325iT-L, your answer to their question is going to be: "Follow me and I'll show you?"

Because of the speed of manufacture, you don't need to waste money on holding stock of beams, trusses and wall panels, you just produce them on an as-and-when-needed basis and while your business begins to expand, we'll be there to support you by sending jobs to you for skeletons sold by FrameUpNow for homes being built in, say, a 250-300-mile radius of you.

If you supply trusses and wall panels to builders, have you thought about supplying steel-frame ones? Doesn't it make financial sense to also build on demand and help accelerate construction outcomes?

Overcoming the biggest hurdle – lack of precision

Many of you will know that one of the previous problems with steel-frame construction was accuracy in the manufacturing of all the parts. With CFS, there is no forgiveness. And that is where FrameUpNow has succeeded while others have failed.

FRAMECAD has created the ultimate machine for producing high-quality CFS parts and FrameUpNow has adopted a design-led approach to perfect the design software. This guarantees that the digital information provided to the

Chapter 12: How to Become a Steel Frame Manufacturer and Collaborator

F325iT-L, 'printing' machine produces inch- or millimetre-perfect results, every single time for each and every frame for our 25 uniquely themed and designed homes. In the simplest of terms, perfect input equals perfect output, which is why FRAMECAD and FrameUpNow have developed such a successful and burgeoning collaborative partnership, one we feel you could benefit from greatly by joining our growing network of collaborators or production partners.

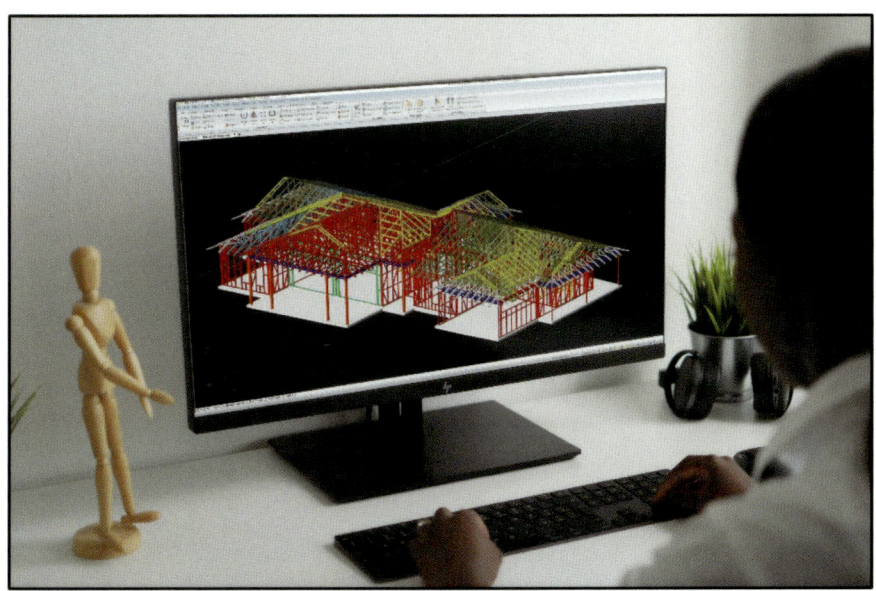

Going not just international, but global

While FrameUpNow is currently making waves in the U.S.A. and creating a national network of production outlets, the company is also in the process of taking the system global. We are able to do this for two reasons.

First, with the purchase of a steel frame, the buyer benefits from a digital file containing the manufacturing details which would be sent to the nearest manufacturing outlet, where the structure is then produced. This means an individual can buy the frame in the U.S.A. and have the frame manufactured in Australia!

Second, we currently have 25 designs for accessory dwelling units (ADUs) or affordable housing. Part of the reason for the global spread of FRAMECAD and FrameUpNow steel-frame housing is the international standards which it meets. These 25 designs for CFS skeletons we provide at FrameUpNow meet all International Building Code (IBC) structural Standards. The IBC is responsible, globally, for ensuring that the quality, safety and sustainability elements of a construction project are strictly adhered to.

Need Financing?

We can recommend attractive options.

Further Reading

For additional information on the FRAMECAD system, we also recommend you download a digital copy of *The Future of Construction: the case for building with cold formed steel.* This book describes how the need for rapid construction not only of ADUs but also of quality buildings is defining the future of construction. The booklet is available in several languages and is definitely well worth reading.

Get in contact with us

We can only scratch the surface on how the global manufacturing system works in this book. If you are intrigued, curious or simply have a specific question you'd like answered, get in contact with us. We are constantly on the lookout for those of you who can recognise the potential in steel-frame residential housing and who relish the prospect of a rewarding challenge

CHAPTER 13: FOR THOSE THAT ARE SUPERSTITIOUS, THERE IS NO CHAPTER 13!

CHAPTER 14: A TYPICAL FRAMEUPNOW SET OF PLANS

32' x 30' Sorin Casita ADU

FOOTPRINT: 32'W X 30'L X 13'-0" H

SQUARE FOOTAGE: 890 SF

OVERALL BUILDING HEIGHT: 13'-0"

PARAPET ROOF: 3:12

WALL HEIGHT: 8'-0"

Chapter 14: A Typical FrameUpNow Set of Plans

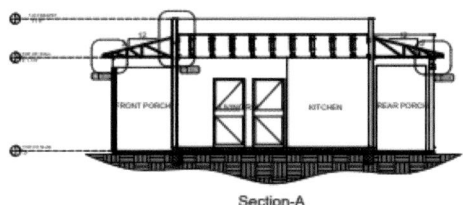

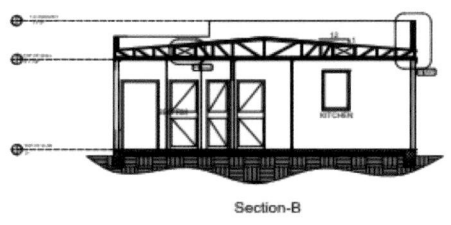

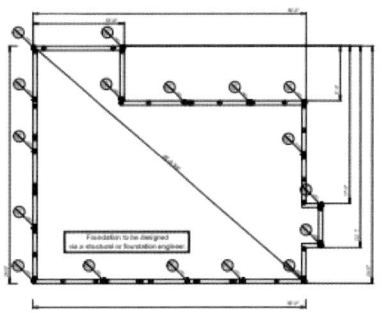

SECTION DETAIL **FOUNDATION**

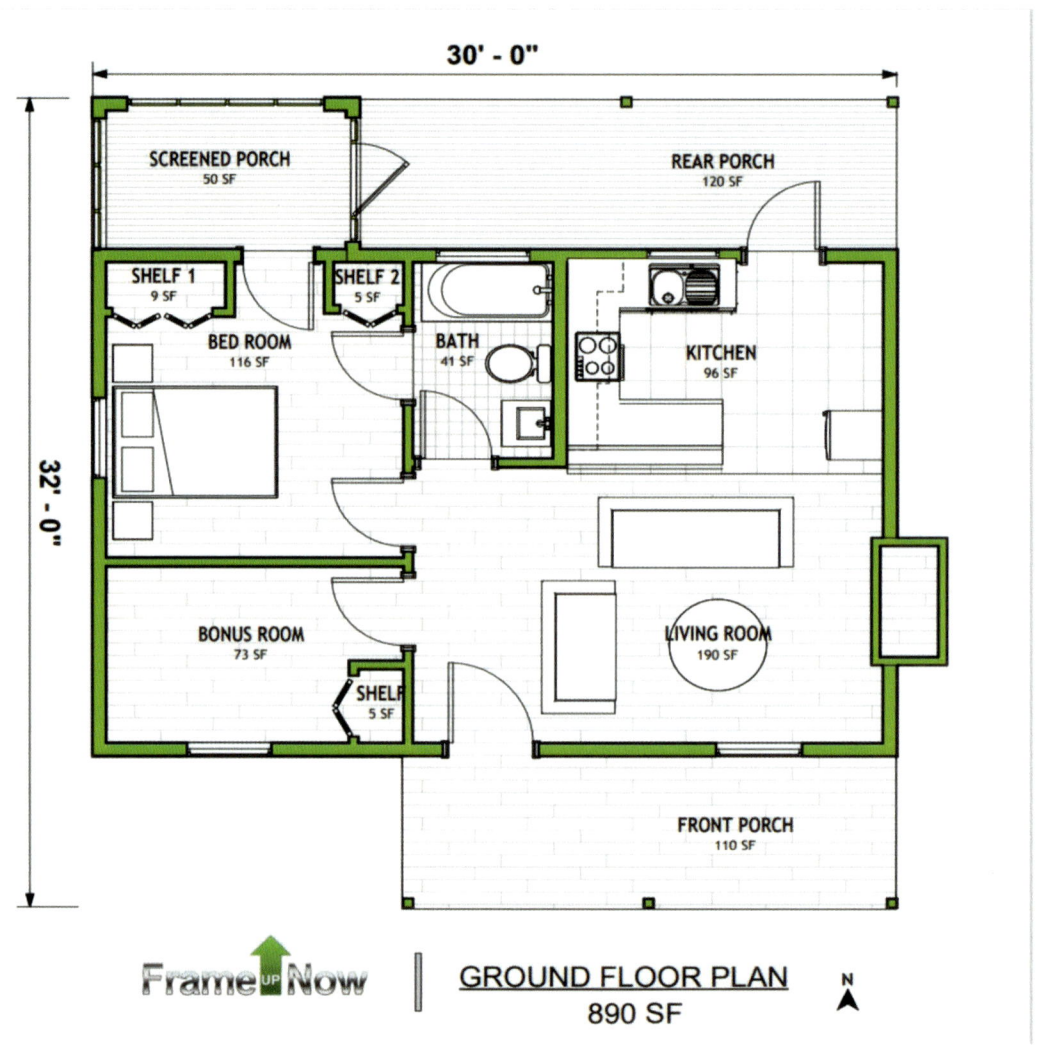

Chapter 14: A Typical FrameUpNow Set of Plans

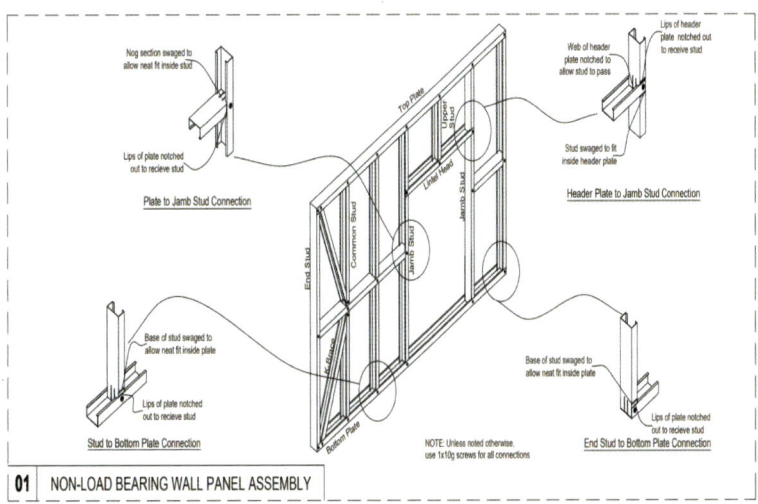

BUIDING DETAILS

Sheet Name	Sheet Name
CS-1	COVER SHEET
GN-1	GENERAL NOTE
S1	FRAMING LAYOUT
S2	PANEL LENGTH
S3	ROOF TRUSS LAYOUT
S4	ELEVATION
S5	SECTIONS VIEW
S6	FRAMING & HOLD-DOWN LAYOUT
S7	FOUNDATION
S8	PANEL LAYOUT & EXTERIOR SNAP SHEET
D1	DETAILS
D2	DETAILS
D3	DETAILS
S9	INTERIOR WALL BLOCKING
S10	LEDGER AND PARAPET CAPPING
S11	TRUSS BLOCKING LAYOUT
S12	PANEL COLOR CODING
FN-1	ROOF BRACING

Plan Name : Sorin Casita_350

BILL OF MATERIAL - PRODUCT LIST

EXTERIOR WALLS

QTY	MATERIAL	SIZE	AREA (SF)	PURPOSE
45	Sheathing	7/16 OSB (4'x8')	1429	Protective covering of outer structural layer
2475	Sheathing Fasteners	Part number		Attach sheathing to the framing of a house
3	Home Wrap	Roll (3'x165')	1443	Covers the exterior sheathing
1285	Home Wrap Fasteners	3/8 Staples		To attach house wrap to the exterior of a building

INTERIOR WALLS

QTY	MATERIAL	SIZE	AREA	PURPOSE
88	Dry Wall	1/2 Inch DW (4'x8')	2824	Protective covering of inner structural layer
2200	Dry Wall Fasteners	Screws		Attach drywall to the framing of a house

ROOFING

QTY	MATERIAL	SIZE	AREA	PURPOSE
2.25	Roofing Felt Paper	Roll (3'x144')	973	Between the roof deck and the shingles
31	Sheathing	7/16 OSB (4'x8')	973	Protective covering of roof structural layer
1525	Sheathing Fasteners	Part number		Attach sheathing to the roof framing

DOOR AND WINDOW

QTY	MATERIAL	SIZE	AREA	LOCATION
2	Door	2'4"x6'8"		Interior
2	Door	2'8"x6'8"		Interior
1	Door	3'9"x6'8"		Interior(By fold)
1	Door	2'5"x6'8"		Interior(By fold)
1	Door	2'1 1/2"x6'8"		Interior(By fold)
1	Door	2'5"x6'8"		Interior
1	Door	3'2"x8'0"		Exterior
1	Door	2'8"x8'0"		Exterior
1	Door	2'10"x8'0"		Exterior
1	Window	3'6"x4'0"		Exterior
1	Window	2'8"x4'0"		Exterior
3	Window	3'2"x6'0"		Exterior

Remark
* All measured areas are in square feet
* All quantities are in number

Chapter 14: A Typical FrameUpNow Set of Plans

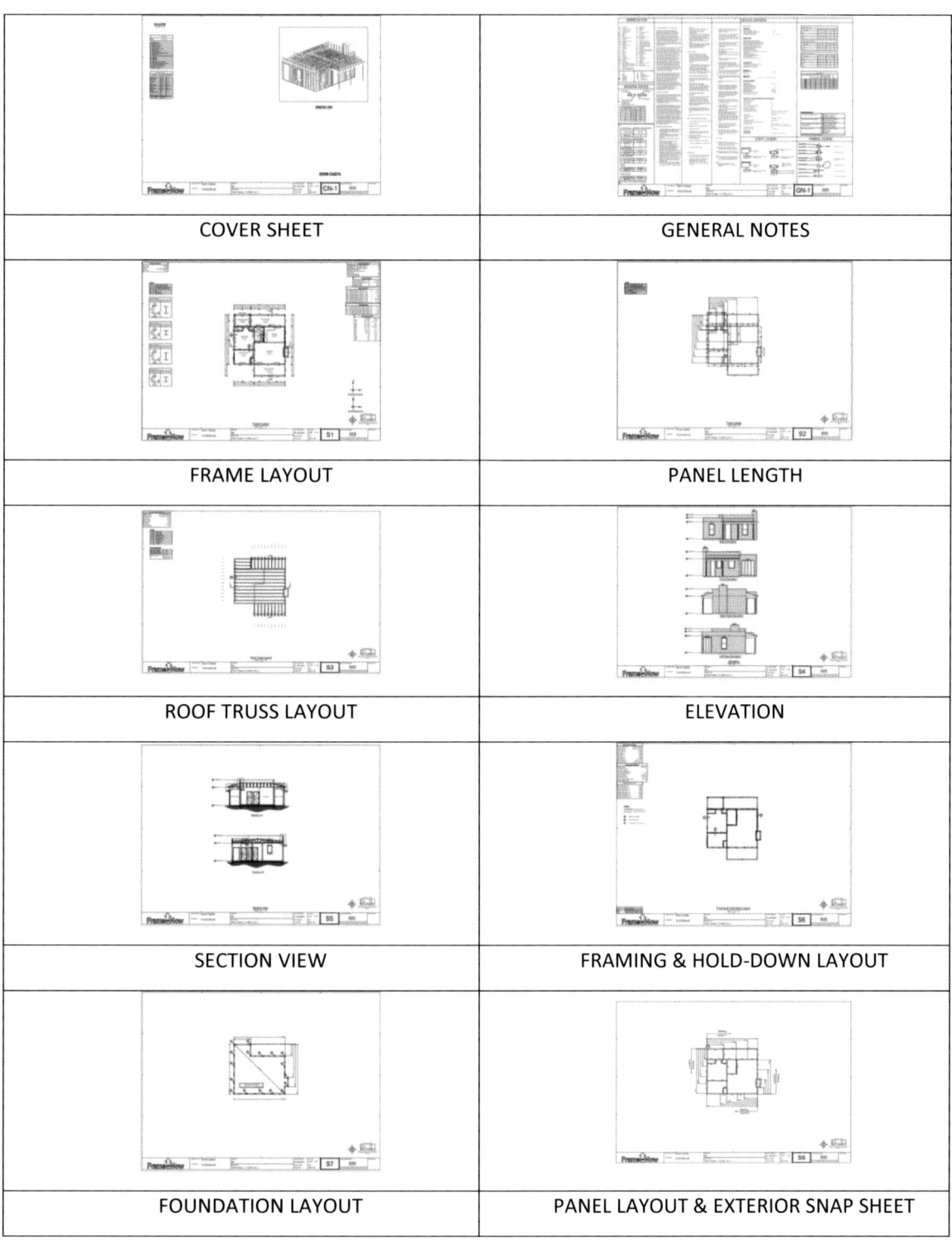

COVER SHEET	GENERAL NOTES
FRAME LAYOUT	PANEL LENGTH
ROOF TRUSS LAYOUT	ELEVATION
SECTION VIEW	FRAMING & HOLD-DOWN LAYOUT
FOUNDATION LAYOUT	PANEL LAYOUT & EXTERIOR SNAP SHEET

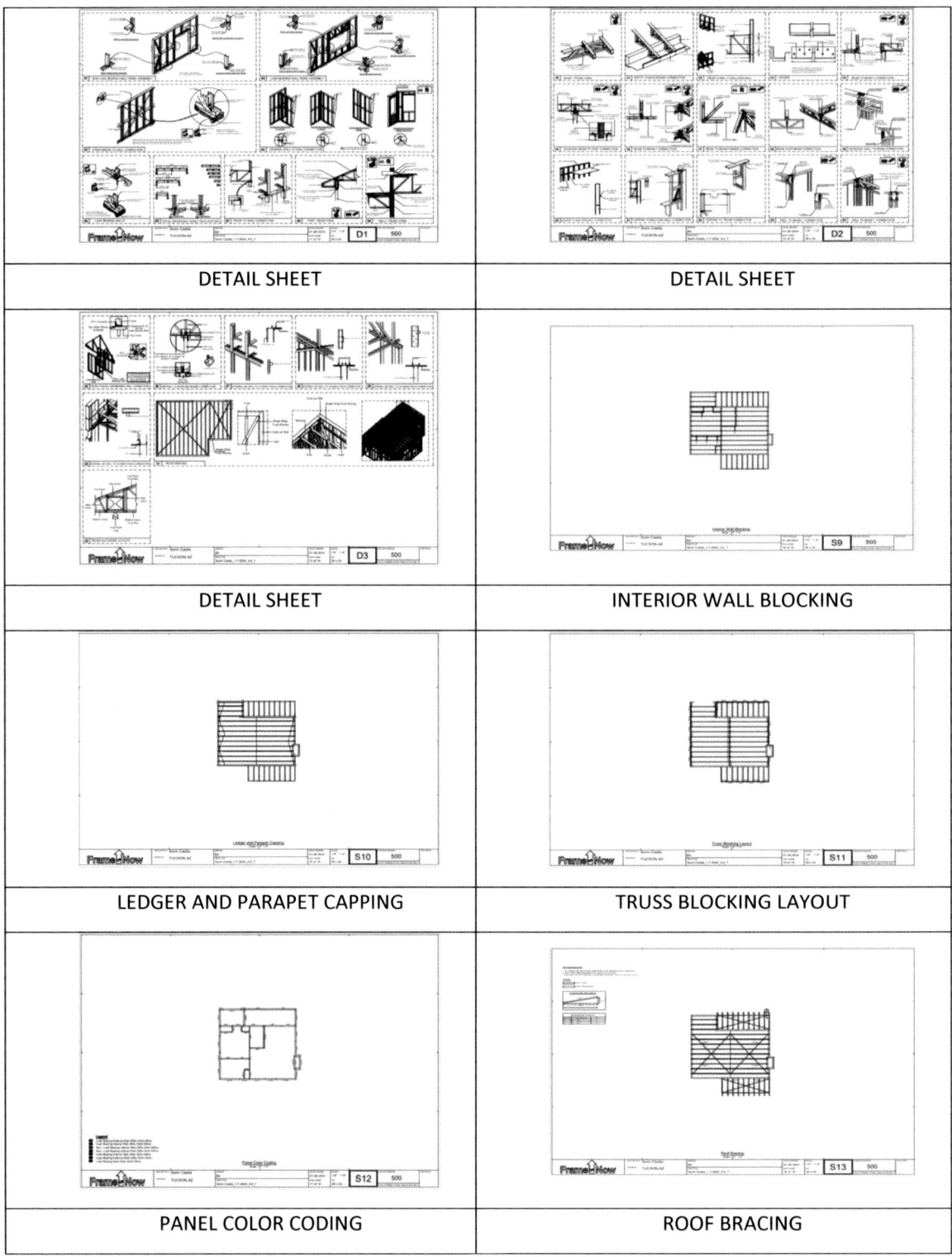

Chapter 14: A Typical FrameUpNow Set of Plans

CHAPTER 15: THE FRAMEUPNOW COLLECTIONS

FrameUpNow Tiny Home Series

The FrameUpNow Tiny Home Series is a collection of Tiny Homes or useful buildings, all based on a 16' x 24' f² / 4.9m x 7.3m foundation.

Tiny Home models include the Cabin/Cottage, Garden House, Man Cave, She Shed, Shop and Garage. Roof pitches are 10/12, 4/12, Flat Modern, or Flat with Parapet walls. The 10/12 pitch provides ample head room to accommodate a 12' x 16' f² loft. A roof pitch is the steepness of a roof expressed as a ratio of inch(es) rise per horizontal foot (or metric equivalent).

Sizes range from 384 f² to 576 f² / 35.7 m² to 53.5 m².

All models are available on a nominal 6 or 4-inch exterior wall panel.

Have it your way! The versatile FrameUpNow Skeleton.

FrameUpNow Affordable Collection

The FrameUpNow Affordable Homes & ADU Series adds additional flexibility in both size and design.

This series of homes include models ranging from 527 f² to 3523 f² / 49 m² to 327 m² and are available in a wide variety of styles to suit most environments.

Area calculations for all homes are "under roof," which includes any porches, patios, or garages.

All styles utilize 4-inch nominal exterior walls and are also available with nominal 6-inch exterior walls.

Tiny Home Roof Designs

10/12 Pitch – 10 wide for 12 vertical

Scissor Truss – Sleeping Loft

FrameUpNow Tiny Home Series

Slight Pitch – within a parapet wall

4/12 Pitch – 4 wide for 12 vertical

FrameUpNow Tiny Home Series

Cabin

Shop

18 variations of the FrameUpNow Tiny Homes

Man Cave

She Shed

Cottage 484 f² 45 m²

ANIMATION OF THIS HOUSE - COTTAGE

Chapter 15: The FrameUpNow Collections

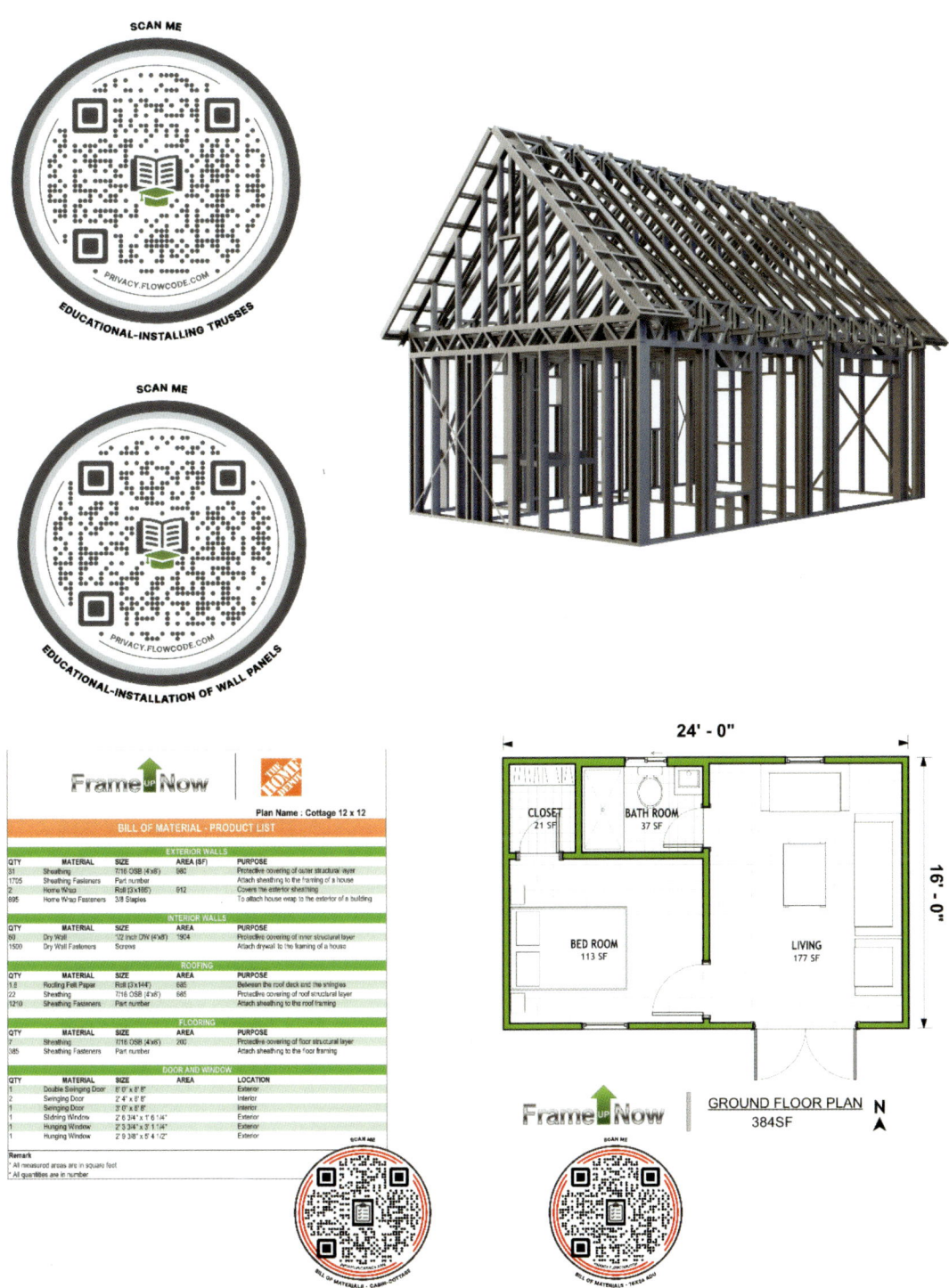

Sorin 890 f² 82.7 m²

Chapter 15: The FrameUpNow Collections

Absolute 732 f² 68 m²

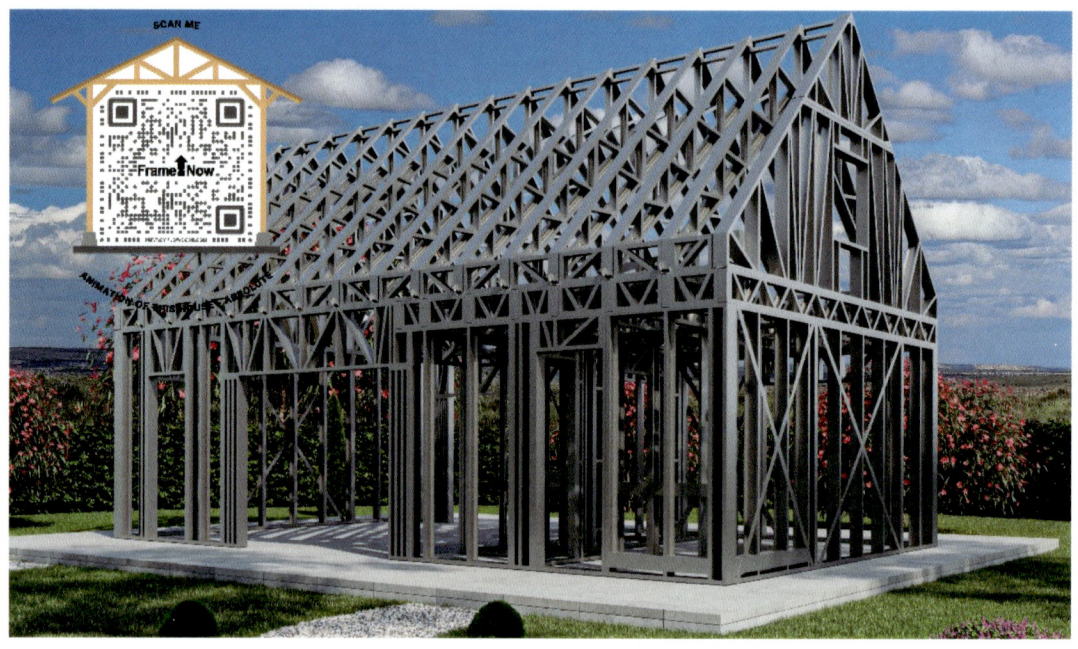

Chapter 15: The FrameUpNow Collections

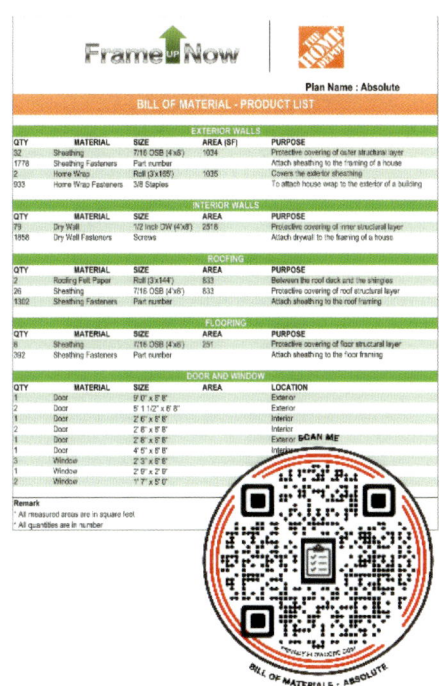

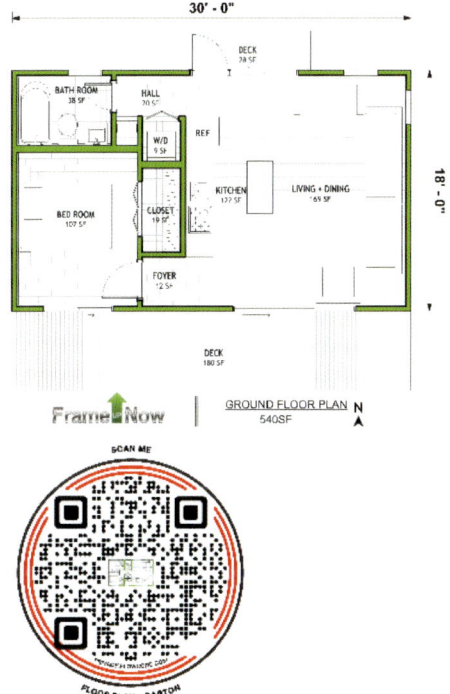

Scout 600 f² 55.75 m²

Chapter 15: The FrameUpNow Collections

Barton 680 f² 63.2 m²

Chapter 15: The FrameUpNow Collections

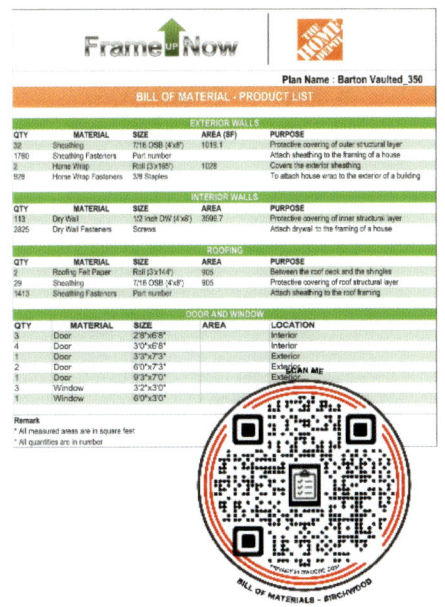

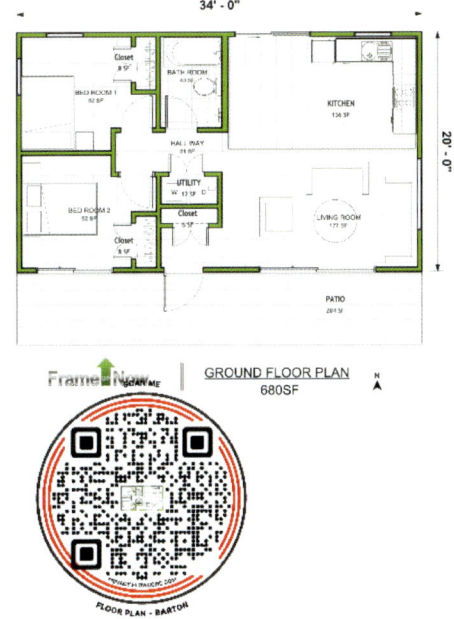

Immense 1141 f² 106 m²

Chapter 15: The FrameUpNow Collections

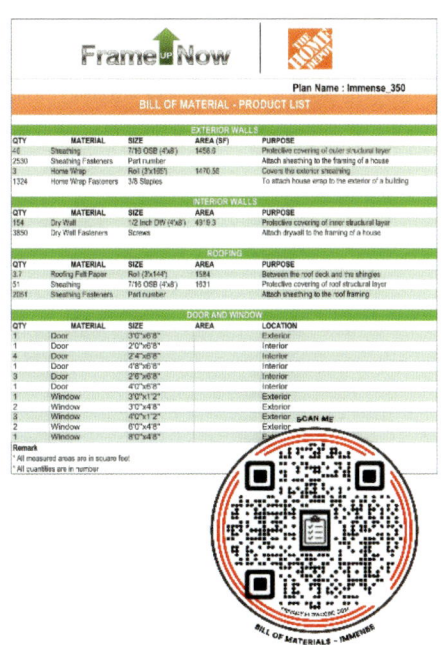

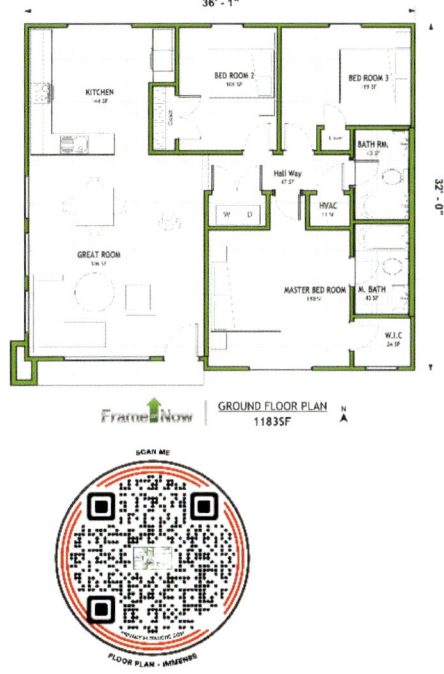

Mulberry 896 f² 83.25 m²

Chapter 15: The FrameUpNow Collections

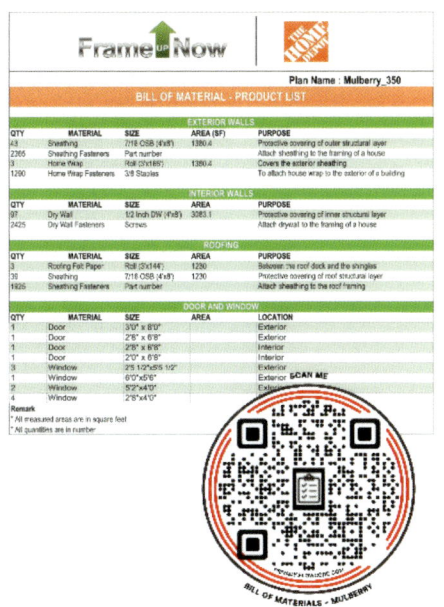

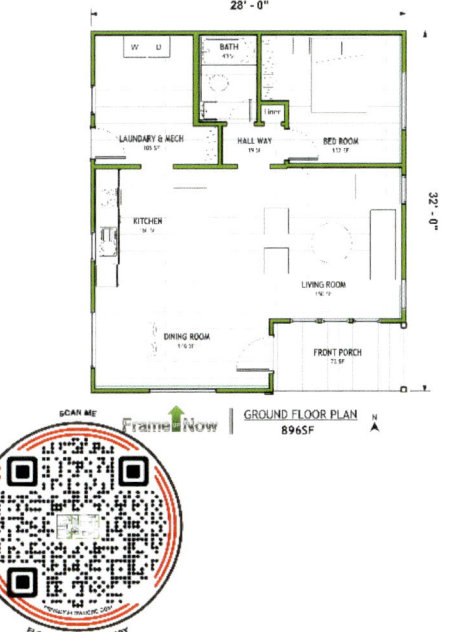

Vallita 800 f^2 74.3 m^2

Chapter 15: The FrameUpNow Collections

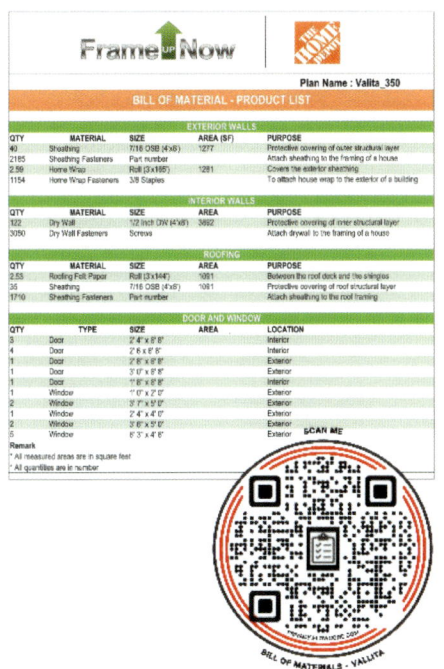

Birchwood 660 f² 61.3 m²

Chapter 15: The FrameUpNow Collections

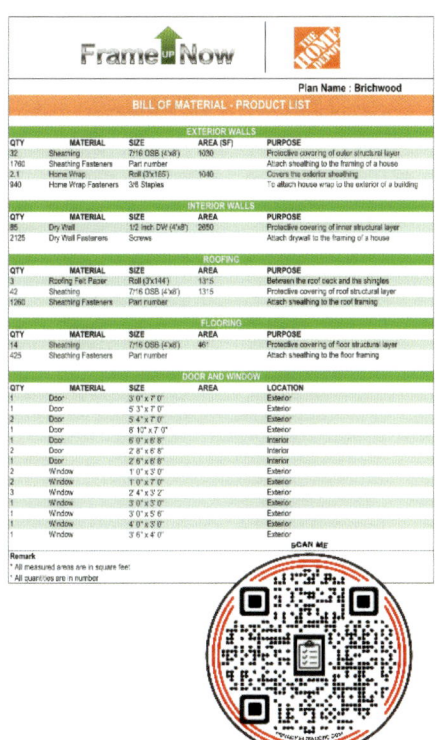

Callahan 864 f² 80.25 m²

Chapter 15: The FrameUpNow Collections

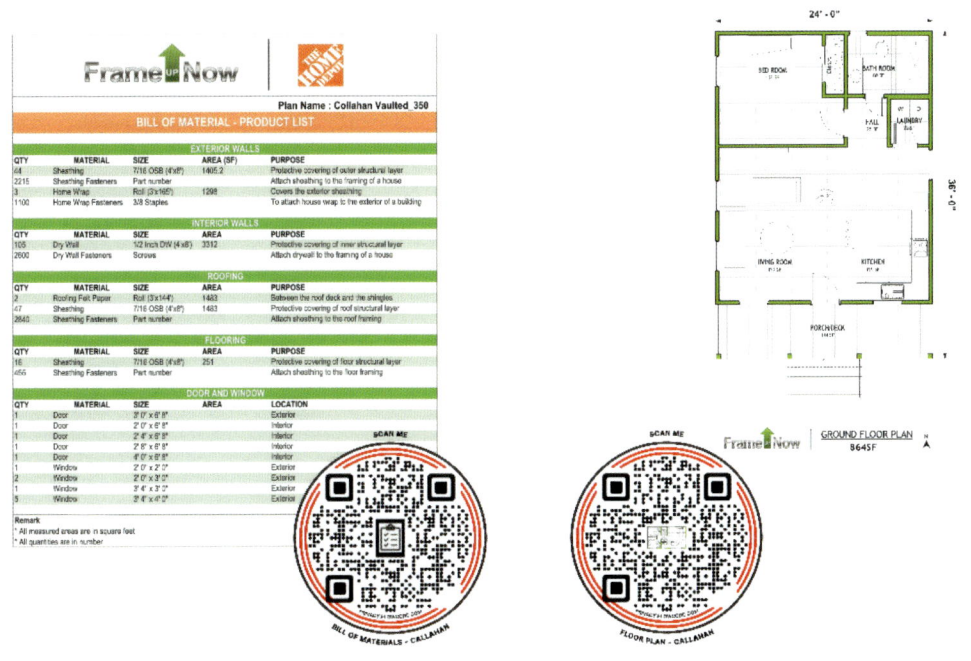

Foxmore 1057 f² 98.2 m²

Chapter 15: The FrameUpNow Collections

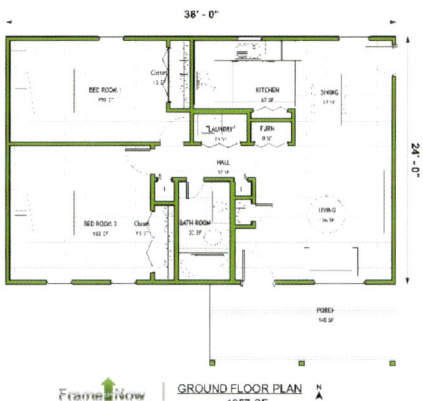

Pacifica 1000 f² 92.9 m²

Chapter 15: The FrameUpNow Collections

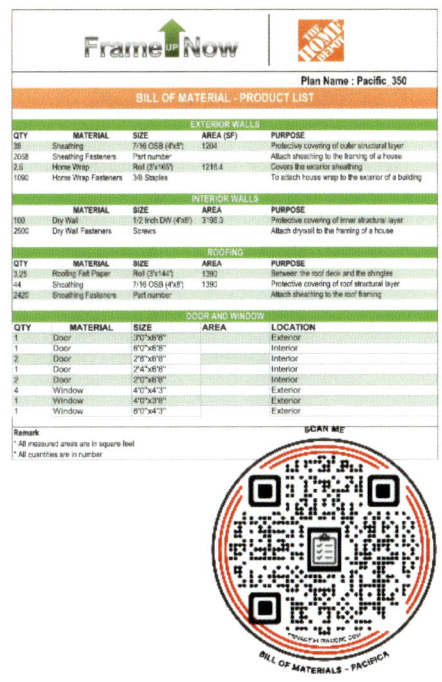

Monroe 1010 f² m² 93

Chapter 15: The FrameUpNow Collections

Russett 990 f² 92 m²

Chapter 15: The FrameUpNow Collections

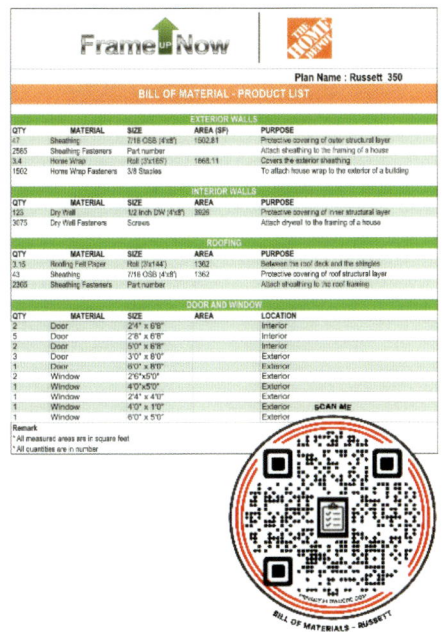

San Diego 1194 f^2 111 m^2

Chapter 15: The FrameUpNow Collections

Lookout 1343 f² 124.8 m²

Chapter 15: The FrameUpNow Collections

Lookout with Garage 2115 f² 196.5 m²

Chapter 15: The FrameUpNow Collections

Rucker 1556 f² 144.5 m²

Chapter 15: The FrameUpNow Collections

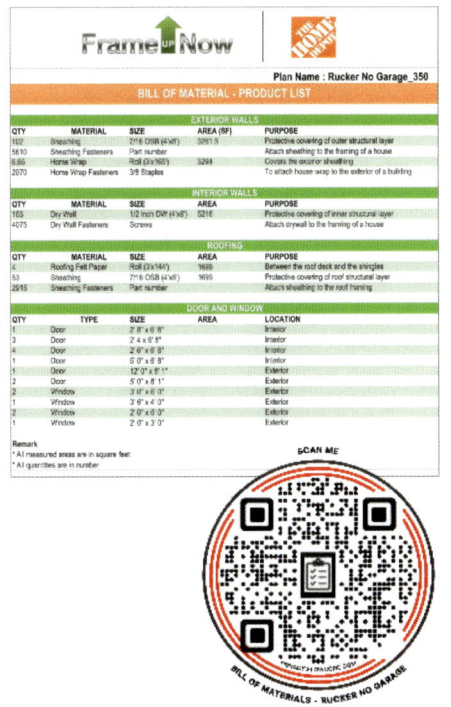

Rucker with Garage 1941 f² 180.3 m²

Chapter 15: The FrameUpNow Collections

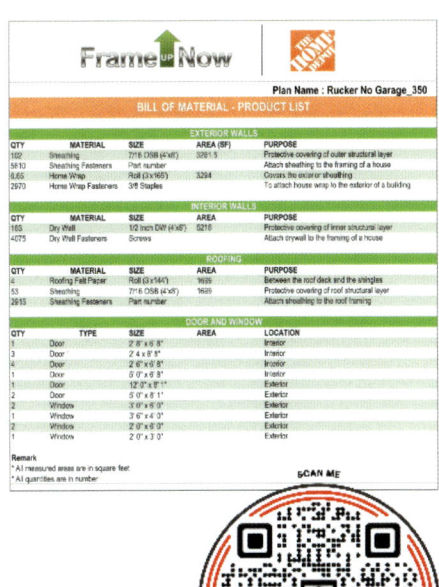

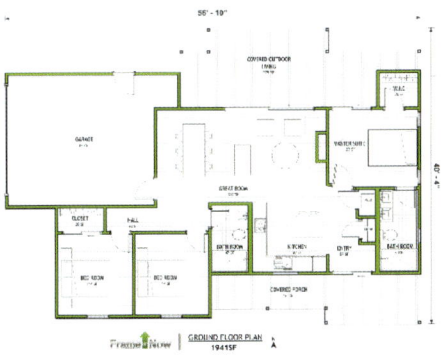

Contempo 1789 f² 166.2 m²

Chapter 15: The FrameUpNow Collections

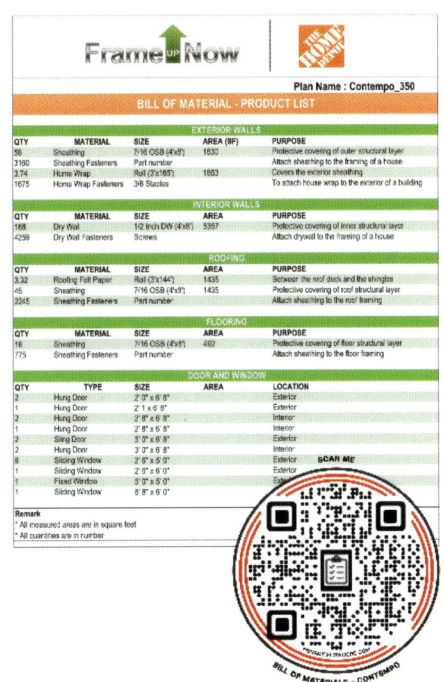

Lilac Modern 527 f² 49 m²

Chapter 15: The FrameUpNow Collections

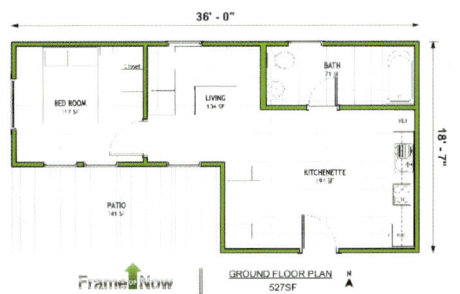

Lilac Parapet 527 f² 49 m²

Chapter 15: The FrameUpNow Collections

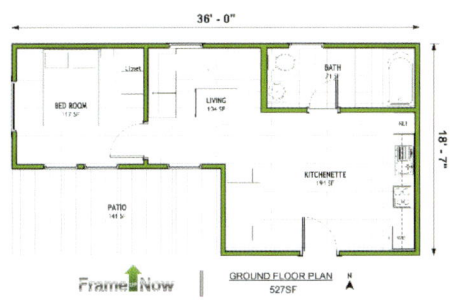

Bungalo 2245 f² 208.6 m²

Chapter 15: The FrameUpNow Collections

Mohave 3523 f² 327.3 m²

Chapter 15: The FrameUpNow Collections

The Versatile FrameUpNow Skeleton

Personalizing Your Steel-Frame Home – "Have it your way"

So, you've decided on the floor plan for your home, the layout of the rooms and any covered outside space. Now comes the fun part where you get to breathe life into the dwelling by choosing the outside finish.

The wonderful thing about these steel-frame units is the choice of numerous designs that will enable you to personalize your home to fit in perfectly with its surroundings.

Do you have a particular style of architecture you like? We have designs with numerous international influences, including French, Japanese, and Italian to name just a few.

Have it your way

What about the roofing material? Do you prefer metal to minimize maintenance, or wood shingles for the aesthetic appeal? How do you want your walls finished? If ease of maintenance is top of your list, a smooth pigmented render will cut out the need for repainting the outside walls every three years. There again, stone or brick can reduce maintenance while adding character to the dwelling.

uPVC, fiberglass, aluminum or timber doors and windows can dramatically affect the overall appearance of a dwelling, and while you look to further reduce maintenance, you can increase individuality.

Affordable housing is affordable, but it doesn't have to look affordable, it can look as good, if not better than many traditional dwellings.

The next page you will see a single home, the "Sorin Skeleton" and 31 suggested exterior themes for the Sorin. That's' why we say, "Have it your way" and localize the home to your environment and taste.

Sorin Desert Modern Original Design

Sorin Bohemian

Sorin Cape Cod

Sorin Costal

Sorin Colonial

Sorin Craftsman

Sorin Eclectic

Sorin French Country (Faites-le à votre façon)

Sorin French Provincial

Sorin Georgian

Sorin Gothic

Sorin Hollywood

Sorin Industrial

Sorin Italianate (Fatela a modo vostro)

Sorin Japanese (Gaweo sak senengmu)

Sorin Lodge

Sorin Minimalist Skeleton

Sorin Minimalist

Sorin Mission Revival (hazlo a tu manera)

Sorin Modern

Sorin Moroccan (أفـعـلـهـا بـطـريـقـتك)

Sorin Prairie

Sorin Ranch

Sorin Ranch Skeleton

Sorin Rustic

Sorin Scandinavian

Sorin Second Empire (በራስህ መንገድ አድርገው)

Sorin Second Empire Skeleton

Sorin Transitional

Sorin Tropical

Sorin Tudor

Sorin Tudor Skeleton

CONTACT US

The intention of this book is to provide you with sufficient information to get a clear understanding of the benefits of CFS affordable steel-frame homes. However, we know that there will likely be questions you want to ask, whether as a potential buyer of one of our 25 individual designs, or because you can see the potential in becoming one of our network of frame manufacturers and collaborators.

The good news is that if you call us, you won't get put through to a call centre, and if you send us an email, you'll get a reply from one of the team, not an AI bot!

Contact Details

Phone: +1-888-864-0184

Address:

FrameUpNow International

1650 Kolb Road Suite 132, Tucson, AZ 85715 USA

Website: https://www.frameupnow.com

Email: inquire@frameupnow.com